Richard Arnold Greene

**Songs From the Psalter**

Richard Arnold Greene

**Songs From the Psalter**

ISBN/EAN: 9783337008819

Printed in Europe, USA, Canada, Australia, Japan

Cover: Foto ©Lupo / pixelio.de

More available books at **www.hansebooks.com**

# Songs from the Psalter

BY

RICHARD ARNOLD GREENE

G. P. PUTNAM'S SONS
NEW YORK & LONDON
The Knickerbocker Press
1899

COPYRIGHT, 1899
BY
RICHARD ARNOLD GREENE
Entered at Stationers' Hall, London

The Knickerbocker Press, New York

To
MY FATHER AND MOTHER
THIS BOOK
IS DEDICATED WITH HEARTY LOVE
BY
THEIR GRATEFUL SON

# CONTENTS

|  | PSALM | PAGE |
|---|---|---|
| A Parable | 49 | 37 |
| A Song of Thanksgiving | 100 | 73 |
| A Song of the Redeemed | 107 | 78 |
| Call to Praise | 67 | 45 |
| Creation's Praise | 148 | 107 |
| Elegy of the Captivity | 137 | 102 |
| Finale |  | 111 |
| God, our Refuge and Strength | 46 | 35 |
| Hallelujah Song | 114 | 85 |
| Jehovah's Exaltation | 97 | 65 |
| Jehovah's Loving-Kindness | 116 | 87 |
| Jehovah's Salvation | 98 | 68 |
| Jehovah's Worthiness of Praise | 95 | 62 |
| Life as a Fleeting Day | 90 | 55 |
| Life's Brief Measure | 39 | 28 |
| Meditation on Simplicity | 131 | 101 |
| Penitence | 51 | 40 |
| Prayer for the Shining of God's Face | 80 | 50 |
| Prelude |  | 1 |
| Song of Home | 127 | 97 |
| Song of the Exile | 120 | 89 |
| Sowing and Reaping | 126 | 96 |
| The Ascendancy of Man | 8 | 7 |
| The Avenging Lord | 144 | 104 |
| The Blessed Home | 128 | 98 |
| The Blessed Life | 1 | 3 |
| The Conquering King | 2 | 5 |
| The Exile's Meditation | 124 | 94 |

## CONTENTS

|  | PSALM | PAGE |
|---|---|---|
| THE EXILE'S PRAYER | 123 | 93 |
| THE GLORIOUS GATES | 24 | 13 |
| THE GOODNESS OF THE LORD | 103 | 75 |
| THE GOOD SHEPHERD | 23 | 12 |
| THE HILLS OF GOD | 121 | 90 |
| THE IDEAL KING | 110 | 83 |
| THE JOYS OF GOD'S HOUSE | 84 | 53 |
| THE KING'S DAUGHTER | 45 | 32 |
| THE KING'S PROTECTOR | 61 | 43 |
| THE LORD'S MAJESTY | 93 | 61 |
| THE LORD, OUR LIGHT AND OUR SALVATION | 27 | 15 |
| THE LORD'S PAVILION | 91 | 58 |
| THE MAN OF HONOR | 15 | 9 |
| THE PENITENT EXILE | 130 | 99 |
| THE PILGRIM SALUTING JERUSALEM | 122 | 91 |
| THE PORTION OF THE RIGHTEOUS | 37 | 23 |
| THE PRAISES OF THE KING | 72 | 47 |
| THE PRAISES OF THE SAINTS | 149 | 109 |
| THE PROMISE OF THE RESURRECTION | 16 | 10 |
| THE REIGNING LORD | 99 | 71 |
| THE STRENGTH OF ZION | 125 | 95 |
| THE STRONG DELIVERER | 34 | 20 |
| THE SURE HIDING-PLACE | 32 | 18 |
| THE TRUE HEART'S DESIRE | 42 | 30 |

# Prelude

Praise ye the Lord.
Praise God in His sanctuary;
Praise Him in the firmament of His power.
Praise Him for His mighty acts:
Praise Him according to His excellent greatness.
Praise Him with the sound of the trumpet:
Praise Him with the psaltery and harp.
Praise Him with the timbrel and dance:
Praise Him with stringed instruments and the pipe.
Praise Him upon the loud cymbals:
Praise Him upon the high=sounding cymbals.
Let everything that hath breath praise the Lord.
Praise ye the Lord.

# SONGS FROM THE PSALTER

## THE BLESSED LIFE

OH! the rich blessedness, the bounteous blessing
    The happy man commands
Whose feet th' ungodly's paths are never pressing,—
    E'en he who never stands

Within the ways where sinners are found treading,
    Beguiling foolish feet,—
Who spurning, dreadeth with a righteous dreading
    To take the scorner's seat:

But in Jehovah's law is his sweet pleasure;
    And in His law doth he
By daytime meditate, and through the measure
    Of night's serenity.

And he shall be like to a tree whose planting
    Is by the water-streams,
That, when its season comes, its fruit is granting,
    Whose leaf, unwithered, gleams.

Whate'er he doth at true success arriveth;
    The wicked are not so;
But like unto the chaff the wind far driveth
    Where'er it lists to go.

So, in the Judgment they shall have no station
    Who wickedly do here;
Nor ever in the righteous congregation
    Shall sinning ones appear.

For all the way of righteous souls He knoweth,—
    The Lord who reigns on high:
But for the way of wicked ones,—it goeth
    The deadly death to die.

# THE CONQUERING KING

WHY thus in tumult are the nations crying?
    Why are the people's thoughts so vain?
The kings of earth their stubborn deeds are plying;
    The rulers counsels entertain

Against the Lord and His Anointed, saying:
    "Their bands asunder let us break;
The cords with which to snare us they're arraying
    To farthest distance let us shake."

How He shall laugh who in the heav'ns is sitting!
    The Lord shall look on them in scorn.
He'll speak to them in anger unremitting,
    In sore displeasure make them mourn:

Yet have I to my holy hill uplifted
    Him whom I chose should reign,—my king,—
Him who with mighty favor hath been gifted—
    Him to Mount Zion did I bring.

I'll tell of the decree:—To me proclaiming,
    The Lord did say: "Thou art my Son;
This day I've Thee begotten, Thee am naming:
    Ask what Thou wilt; it shall be done—

"Ask, and I 'll make Thee heir of all the nations;
  Earth's farthest parts shalt Thou possess:
With iron rod Thou 'lt scatter their foundations,
  And dash them in chaotic mess,

"Like vessels of the potter, crushed and broken."—
  Now, therefore, be ye wise, O kings:
Ye judges of the earth, be guided by this token
  Which highest wisdom to you brings.

Oh, serve the Lord with fear, with fear rejoicing—
  Kiss ye the Son lest wroth He be,
And from the way ye fall, nor hear Him voicing
  The pardon which He offers free.

For soon will flame His wrath in direful burning—
  How wonderfully they are blest
Who to the Lord in trustfulness returning
  Shall find in trusting Him their rest!

# THE ASCENDENCY OF MAN

How excellent, Lord, O Lord, our Lord,
   In all the earth 's Thy name!
Thy glory Thou hast shed abroad
   Above the heavens' frame—
From babes' and sucklings' mouths hast Thou
   Firmly established strength,
Because of those that fight Thee now,
   That Thou might'st still at length
Him who is hostile found and him
Who worketh plots of vengeance grim.

When I behold Thy heavens high,—
   The work Thy fingers planned,—
The moon and all the starry sky
   Appointed by Thy hand—
Oh, what is man that Thou should'st hold
   Him always in Thy mind?
And to the son of man of old
   Why comest Thou so kind?
Just less than angels him hast made,
With fame and honor's crown arrayed.

Him madest Thou like unto kings
   Thy handiwork to keep;

Under his feet hast put all things,—
  All oxen and all sheep—
Yea, and the beasts which tread the grass—
  Bird, fish, where'er they be—
Whatever kinds of creature pass
  Through the deep paths of sea;
How excellent Thy name is found,
O, Lord, our Lord, the earth around!

## THE MAN OF HONOR

JEHOVAH, who shall be residing
    Within Thy Tabernacle blest?
Uplifted, in sweet peace abiding,
    Who in Thy Holy Hill shall rest?
He who in upright walks takes part,
    Who righteousness is ever seeking,—
He who within his very heart
    The words of truthfulness is speaking;

Whose tongue shall never move in slander,
    Who doth no evil to his friend,
Nor for a neighbor's hurt doth pander,—
    By whom he that to vice doth tend
Is held in no esteem at all;—
    But on all them who God are fearing
His marks of signal honor fall,
    Before the face of man appearing.

He that to his own hurt is swearing,
    He who is found unchanging still;
He who, in nowise, shall be caring
    With usury his purse to fill;
And he who takes no recompense
    Against the innocent around him:—
For him who doeth thus,—a fence
    Of true security shall bound him.

# THE PROMISE OF THE RESURRECTION

KEEP me, O God; I trust in Thee—
    Unto Jehovah I have cried:
"My Lord, Thou dost belong to me;
    With Thee alone my good doth bide."
As for the saintly company
    That on this earth of ours reside,—
With excellence their souls are bright,
In whom, behold all my delight.

Their sorrows shall increase apace
    That for another god exchange
Jehovah: I will find no place
    For off'ring their oblation strange
Of drink and blood; for such disgrace
    Mine altar I will ne'er arrange;
Nor will I with my lips proclaim
Their faithless and rebellious name.

The Lord of mine inheritance
    And of my cup is the blest share;
My lot Thou givest maintenance;
    My pleasant lines Thou dost prepare;
To goodly gifts I shall advance,—
    An heritage supremely fair—
I 'll bless the Lord who gives me light;
My reins instruct me in the night.

I 've ever placed before mine eyes
   The Lord: since He 's at my right hand
I shall be moved not any wise—
   So gladly doth my heart expand.
My glory in great joy doth rise;
   My flesh shall dwell in a safe land:
For Thou wilt not desert my soul
To languish in the dark Sheol.

Nor wilt Thou let thy Holy One
   The pitfall of corruption see;
Life's path that shineth as the sun
   Thou graciously wilt show to me.
With Thee, our joy but scarce begun
   Shall bloom in full felicity—
At Thy right hand, in bounteous store
Are pleasures found for evermore.

# THE GOOD SHEPHERD

MY Shepherd is the Lord of all;
    No want unto my lot shall fall
  While I have Him beside me.
He makes me rest in pastures green,
And where still waters flow between
  He graciously doth guide me.

My soul to health He doth restore;
In paths of right He goes before,
  And leadeth, ever near me—
Yea, though I walk within Death's vale
No evil thing shall make me quail;
  Thy rod and staff,—they cheer me.

Before my foes Thou dost appoint
My table; and my head anoint;
  My cup is still outgiving.
Goodness and mercy 'tend my days,
God's House the goal of all my ways,
  Where I'll be ever living.

# THE GLORIOUS GATES

THE earth unto the Lord belongs,—
    The fulness of its life and air;
The world, and all that in it throngs,
    All they who have their dwelling there;
He makes it for the seas a crown;
Upon the floods hath set it down.

Who shall ascend Jehovah's Hill?
    Who stand within His Holy Place?
He whose clean hands have wrought no ill,
    Whose heart is pure before God's face.
His soul to pride is ne'er upborne;
Deceitfully he hath not sworn.

To him a blessing shall come down
    Straight from the Lord; with righteousness
The God of saving power will crown
    Him, and through all his days will bless.
This is an earnest seeking race;
They seek, O Jacob's God, Thy face.

Ye Gates, your heads uplift o'er sin!
    Ye everlasting Doors, arise!
The King of Glory shall come in—
    Who is this King in glory-guise?

He is the Lord of strength and might,
Whom none can vanquish in the fight.

Ye Gates, your heads uplift o'er sin!
　Ye everlasting Doors, arise!
The King of Glory shall come in—
　Who is this King in glory-guise?
The Lord whom hosts adoring view,—
He is the King of Glory true.

# THE LORD, OUR LIGHT AND OUR SALVATION

JEHOVAH is my shining Light,
    And my salvation He—
By whom shall I be filled with fright?
    The Lord my life doth free,
The Lord its strength for doing right—
    Who fearful maketh me?

When wicked ones, swift drawing near,
    Mine enemies, my foes,
To eat my flesh, did all appear
    They stumbled, nor arose;
Though on before, and in my rear,
    A camping host oppose,

No fear shall dwell within my heart;
    Though war against me rise,
Then confidence shall be my part;—
    One boon, in any wise,
From all Jehovah's bounteous mart
    I set before mine eyes;—

For this I'll diligently press:
    That I indeed may dwell
Within God's House of righteousness,

While I life's days shall tell,—
To see the Lord's own beauty, yes,
His Temple's vows to swell.

For in the day of trouble He
Me in his Tent will hide;
In His own Dwelling's secrecy
He'll cause me to abide—
Unto a Rock that cannot flee
My wayward feet He'll guide.

And now my head shall He lift high
Above my foes around;
And at His Shrine, with joyful cry,
I'll be with off'rings found—
I'll sing, yea, songs of praise will I
Make to the Lord resound.

Lord, when my voice is crying, hark;
Have mercy upon me;
My prayers for speedy answer mark—
When Thou did'st say: "Seek ye
My face," my heart said from the dark:
"Thy face, Lord, would I see."

Hide not afar from me Thy face,
Nor, angered, put away
Thy servant; Thou in mighty grace
Hast been my help and stay;
Leave nor forsake me in this place,
My saving God, I pray.

When father and when mother, too,
    Forsake me, then the Lord
Will take me up: show to my view
    Thy way—to me afford
A pathway plain my journey through;
    My foes are all abroad.

Unto their will give me not o'er;
    False witnesses arise
Against me; cruel words they store;
    They breathe out cruel lies;
I should have fainted long before
    Did I not e'en surmise

That I God's goodness should behold
    Within the immortal Land—
Wait on the Lord; be strong and bold;
    Thine heart with His own hand
He 'll strengthen with His strength of old:
    Wait on the Lord's command.

## THE SURE HIDING-PLACE

HOW blest is he who winneth for
    Transgression, pardon free,—
Whose sin, indeed, is covered o'er!
    How truly blest is he
To whom the Lord doth nevermore
    Impute iniquity,—

Within whose spirit is no guile!—
    When I held silence deep
My bones, they waxéd old the while;
    For roaring did I keep
All day;—grief on me Thou did'st pile,
    Or waking, or asleep,

To summer drought my moisture passed;
    To Thee my guilt told I;
Concerning sin that held me fast
    To Thee I did not lie.
" I will confess," said I, at last,
    " My sin to God Most High."

And Thou, my Lord, did'st pardon then
    My sin's iniquity—
For this Thy gracious goodness, when

## THE SURE HIDING-PLACE

Discernéd Thou may'st be,
Let him who godliness doth ken
  Uplift his prayers to Thee.

Sure, when the water-floods o'erflow,
  O'er him they shall not throng—
My hiding-place from grief, I know
  Thou 'lt keep me all life long;
Around me Thou wilt oft bestow
  The glad deliverance song.

I will instruct thee, make thee find
  The only righteous way;
And where Mine eye thy heart can bind
  I 'll counsel thee each day—
Be not like them who lack thy mind,
  Horse, mule, who naught can say,

Who must with bit and bridle strong
  Be held where'er they go,
Else, they will turn from thee all wrong;
  The wicked souls shall know
Much grief—to them shall sorrows throng:—
  He trusting God 's not so,—

Mercy shall compass him around;
  Be gladness your life-chart,—
God's gladness; in joys that abound,
  Ye righteous souls, take part;
And shout for joy, all ye who 're found
  To be of upright heart.

# THE STRONG DELIVERER

THE Lord at all times I will bless;
    His praise my mouth shall never leave;
The Lord shall be the boast, no less,
    That my rejoicing soul shall weave.

The meek shall hear it and have joy—
    Oh, magnify the Lord with me;
Together let us songs employ;
    His name by us exalted be.

I sought the Lord; His answer came,
    And set me free from all my fears;
They looked to Him, and lighter frame
    Succeeded to their grief and tears.

Their trustful faces nevermore
    Shall dire confusion meet again;
This poor man cried in anguish sore,—
    God heard, and banished all his pain.

The Angel of the Lord His tent
    Binds round the souls who fear His name;
And when with terror they are rent
    From Him deliverance they can claim.

## THE STRONG DELIVERER

Oh, taste and see the goodness true
   That in our gracious Lord resides—
Blest is the man who Him can view
   With trustfulness that e'er abides.

Oh, fear the Lord, all ye His saints;
   They shall not want who Him do fear;
The lion's young, with direful plaints,
   Will make their lack of food appear,

But they who seek the Lord indeed
   Shall never want for one good thing—
Come, children, unto me pay heed;
   To fear the Lord you will I bring.

Who 's he that doth long life desire?
   Loves many days, good things to see?—
Thy tongue from evil keep entire,
   And let thy lips from guile be free;

Depart from evil, and do right;
   Seek peace, and ever it pursue;
The Lord the righteous keeps in sight,
   His ears their cry are open to.

Jehovah setteth fast his face
   Against the evil-doers all,
That on the earth may be no place
   Where any one shall them recall.

The righteous cried; Jehovah heard,
   And from their troubles set them free;
The Lord the broken heart doth gird;
   He saveth such as contrite be.

The righteous hath pains manifold;
  Him from them all delivereth
The Lord.　He all his bones doth hold;
  Not one of them is broken.　Death

Shall evil make the wicked's goal;
  And they that hate the good shall be
Condemned.　The Lord redeems the soul
  Of those who serve Him faithfully.

And none of them who place their trust
  In Him, Jehovah, Lord of all,—
The Lord of Love, the True, the Just,—
  Shall into condemnation fall.

# THE PORTION OF THE RIGHTEOUS

FRET not thyself because of those
    Who evil do, and good oppose;
  Nor ever envious be thou
'Gainst them that work unrighteousness.
They soon shall feel the sickle's stress
    Like to the grass that waveth now;
Like the green herb shall they be dried—
Do thou in thine own Lord confide;
  With goodness all thy days endow.

Dwell in the land; and follow near
On faithfulness: have blessed cheer
    In Him, Jehovah, Lord Most High;
Thy heart's desires He 'll thee afford.
Commit thy way unto the Lord;
    Forevermore on Him rely,
And He shall bring it to thy sight—
He 'll make thy righteousness like light,
    Thy judgment like the noonday sky.

Be still before the Lord; for Him
Wait patiently, though sight be dim;
    Do thou not fret thyself at all
For him who prospereth in his way;
For him who bringeth to the day
    Devices that for sin appal.

From anger cease, and wrath forsake;
Fret not thyself, it sin doth make—
  Those doing ill to death shall fall.

But those that wait upon the Lord
The land shall win, so fair and broad:
  For yet, indeed, a little while
And wicked souls shall be no more:
Yea, shalt thou in thy thought explore,
  With diligence, the place of guile,
And it, once mighty, shall not be;
But meek ones shall their portion see
  Unrolled to earth's most distant isle.

They shall delight themselves in peace
Whose fair abundance shall not cease;
  The wicked plotteth 'gainst the just
And gnasheth with his teeth on him—
For him the Lord hath laughter grim,
  He marks his swift return to dust;
The wicked have the sword outdrawn,
And they have bent their bow in scorn
  The poor and needy low to thrust;

To slay them of the upright part—
Their sword shall enter their own heart;
  Through breakage shall their bows have harm,—
The mite the righteous hath is more
Than wicked souls' abundant store,—
  Broken shall be each wicked arm.
On true hearts help the Lord bestows;
The days of perfect ones He knows;
  Their lot shall be an endless charm.

In evil times no shame they 'll know;
In famine satisfied they 'll go;
   But wicked ones shall perish all,
And those who 'gainst Jehovah fight
Shall be as pastures richly dight;
   They shall consume; in smoke they 'll fall—
The wicked borrows, not to pay;
But righteous souls in gracious way
   Bestow their gifts, both great and small.

For such as blest of Him do stand
Shall come to heirship of the land;
   But they who have His curse shall pay
In death; of God established are
Man's goings, be they near or far,
   And He delighteth in his way—
Fallen, not quite cast down he 'll be;
For him the Lord upholdeth free,
   And makes His hand his stay.

I have been young, and now am old,
Yet he who doth the right uphold
   Forsaken have I never found,
Nor begging for their bread his seed:
All day he takes most gracious heed
   And lends; his seed 's with blessing crowned.
Depart from every evil way,
And practise good from day to day,
   And dwell for aye on thine own ground.

For judgment doth Jehovah love,
Nor doth He from His throne above

Forsake them who are sanctified.
Preserved forevermore are they,
But for the wicked's seed,—away,
  Cut off, it will no more abide;
The righteous shall the land receive,—
Their heritage, no more to leave,—
  Their dwelling, with Thy grace supplied.

The mouth of him who righteous is
Of wisdom talks, 't is surely his;
  Concerning judgment speaks his tongue—
His God's own law is in his heart;
No steps of his shall sliding start.
  In watching have the wicked hung
Beside the righteous everywhere;
And seek they with most earnest care
  That with the death-pang he be stung.

The Lord within the wicked's hand
Will not permit just souls to stand;
  For them, when judged, condemn will He:
Wait on the Lord, and keep his way
And thee shall He exalt one day
  The land's inheritor to be.
When all cut off the wicked are
Naught from thine eyes the sight shall bar
  Of their most dread extremity.

The wicked in great power I 've seen,
Wide-spreading, like a tree that 's green,
  Implanted in its native soil;

Yet passed he by; lo! was no more;
Yea, sought I him behind, before,
   But found him not for all my toil.
Mark him that perfect is; behold
The upright one; for when he 's old
   For pain, shall peace be his bright foil.

As for transgressors, they shall all
Together to destruction fall;
   Cut off shall be their latter end.
Saved are the righteous by the Lord;
He, strong, in trouble them will ward;
   The Lord with help doth them attend,
He rescueth their souls from death;
E'en from the evil doer's breath,
   Since Him they 've asked, them to defend.

## LIFE'S BRIEF MEASURE

I SAID: "Unto my ways I will take heed,
  That with my tongue I may commit no sin;
  My mouth I'll keep a bridle fast within,
While wicked ones before me do proceed."

With silence dumb, I even held my peace
    From good; and then, indeed, was stirred my
      woe;
  My heart with burning inward heat did glow,
The flame arose, nor did my musing cease.

Then said my tongue: "Lord, make me know mine
    end,
  And what the measure of my days may be;
  Make me acquainted with my frailty;
As handbreadths, see, Thou dost my days extend,

"And mine age is as nothing in Thy sight—
  Surely, at best estate, man's but a breath;
  In shadow, surely, each man travelleth;
Surely, in vain they're thrown in restless plight.

" He heaps on high, and knows not who shall gain
   His wealth: and now, Lord, what do I wait for?
   My hope 's in Thee; save me from my sins sore;
Let me not be reproach of fools so vain.

" Dumb was I, nor did I my mouth unclose,
   Because Thou did'st it: be my heart not rent;
   Consumed am I; my strength Thy blow hath
      spent,
The blow whose sharpness only Thine hand knows.

" When, with rebukes, for sin Thou chidest man,
   His beauty Thou dost make to pass away
   Like to a moth; but vanity, I say,
Is every being in this mortal span.

" O Thou, Jehovah, listen to my prayer,
   And lend Thine ear unto mine earnest cry;
   Hold not Thy peace, when I with tears shall sigh;
For I with Thee do as a stranger fare,—

" Sojourner, as my fathers were before.
   Oh, spare Thou me, that I, indeed, at length
   In Thy great mercy may recover strength,
Before I go far hence and be no more."

# THE TRUE HEART'S DESIRE

AS for the water-brooks the hart is panting,
    So pants, indeed, my soul, O God, for Thee;
My soul, with thirst, from depths of its implanting
    Still longeth God, the living God to see.

When shall I come, before my God appearing?—
    My tears have been my meat by day and night,
While in continuance their cry I 'm hearing,—
    "Where is thy God?" they say, through dark and light.

These things I mind, my soul in me outpouring,—
    How I when marching onward with the throng,
Unto God's House led multitudes adoring
    On holy day, with voice of joy and song.

Oh! soul of mine, why art thou downward bending,
    And why dost keep within me toilsome quest?
Hope thou in God; His praises I 'll be blending
    For health that on His countenance doth rest.

My soul, O God, within me takes low station:—
    Thus I remember Thee from Jordan's land,
The Hermons, and from Mizar's elevation—
    Deep calleth deep—Thy waterspouts command.

Thy waves have compassed me and many a billow;
Yet God, by day, His kind love will ordain;
And all night long His song shall be my pillow—
A prayer to God who o'er my life doth reign.

To God who is my Rock will I be saying:
"Why hast Thou me forgot; why do I mourn,
Because of my foes' malice on me weighing?"
As though a sword my bones had crushed and torn.

My foes reproach me, while they're ever crying:
"Where is thy God?"—Why art cast down, my soul?
And why art thou within me restless sighing?
Do thou upon the Lord thy burden roll.

In Him do thou have hope that shall not perish;
For I shall yet to Him my praises sing.
My countenance's health is He; He'll cherish
His heavy-hearted child, my God, my King!

## THE KING'S DAUGHTER

WITH a goodly matter my heart doth overflow;
I speak; upon the King do I my work bestow,
   My tongue's the pen of one who readily doth write.
Thou fairer art than all the children of man's race;
Upon thy parted lips is poured the dew of grace,—
   So thou art blest of God, forever, in His sight.

Gird, gird thy sword upon Thy thigh, O Mighty One,—
Thy glory and Thy majesty, Thy race to run;
   And in Thy majesty all prosperously ride,
Because of truth and peace and righteousness,
And Thy right hand upon Thee terrors shall impress,
   Thine arrows sharp the people fell on every side.

Within the heart of the King's enemies are they—
Thy throne O God 's forever through th' eternal day;
   Sceptre of equity 's the sceptre of Thy reign—
Thou hast loved righteousness and hated wicked ways.

So God, thy God, hath thee anointed for all days,
  With gladness' oil above the comrades in thy
    train.

Myrrh, aloes, cassia, scent the robes wherewith
    thou 'rt clad;
From ivory courts stringed instruments have made
    thee glad;
  Among thy women honored high kings' daughters
    are,
Upon thy right doth stand in Ophir's gold the
    Queen.
Hearken, oh! Daughter, mark; incline thine ear
    serene!—
Forget thy people loved, thy father's house afar.

So shall the King thy beauty ardently desire,
For He is thine own Lord; then worship Him, nor
    tire—
  The Tyrian daughter there for thee a gift shall
    hold.
The rich among the race thy favor shall entreat;
The Daughter of the King with glory is replete,
  Within the inner court—her robes are wrought
    in gold.

In broidered work shall she be led unto the King;
The virgins fair, her near companions following,
  Shall be, each one, into Thy gracious presence
    brought—
With gladness and rejoicing shall they all be led;

They 'll enter where He dwells who is their King
    and Head—
  His palace gleaming with a glory passing thought.

Where once thy fathers were, now shall thy children
    stand,
Whom thou in all the regions of the earth's broad
    land
  Shalt call to prince's station—this their lot in
    store.
Through all the generations I 'll make thy name to
    live
In lasting memory; so shall the people give
  Thanks unto thee for ever and for evermore.

# GOD, OUR REFUGE AND STRENGTH

GOD is our Refuge and our Strength unfailing,—
  A very present help in pain;
Therefore will we not fear, earth's changes hailing,
  And though the deep sea's heart should strain,

Invaded by the hills of mighty presence,—
  Although its waves should troubled roar,
Though fearful at its swell and effervescence,
  Tremble and quail the mountains hoar.

There is a River pure, whose streams soft swelling
  With gladness fill the City of our God,—
The Holy Place, within the tents of dwelling
  Of the Most High, in light adored.

His voice He raised; earth melted at its thunder;
  The Lord of Hosts with us resides;
The God of Jacob is our High Tower, under
  Whose covering my soul abides.

Come; be our Lord Jehovah's work beholding,—
  What desolation on the earth
He makes; yet bids He wars to cease, enfolding
  The earth with joy, since Peace hath birth.

He breaks the bow, and casts the spear in sunder;
  The chariots, in His fire abroad
He burns: in reverential awe and wonder
  Be still, and know that I am God.

Exalted will I be in every nation;
  Upon the earth I 'll be made high.
The Lord of Hosts is with us—sure salvation;
  E'en Jacob's God, to whom we fly.

## A PARABLE[1]

HEAR this, all ye peoples, hear!
All who dwell on earth, give ear!
Low and high, and rich and poor,
Wisdom shall my mouth assure;—
   And my heart's meditation
How to understand shall be;
Parable shall wait on me;
On the harp I 'll open wide
Word of mine that doth abide
   Where Darkness holds her station.

Wherefore should I fearful stand
In the days when Ill 's at hand;
When dark Sin upon my heels
Round and round about me wheels?—
   They who on wealth are standing
Boast themselves of riches vast—
None of them, indeed, at last
Can redeem his brother lost,
Nor to God give back the cost
   His ransom is demanding.

---

[1] For the title of this song, as well as for those of a few that follow, the author acknowledges his indebtedness to suggestions derived from Prof. Richard G. Moulton's work, *The Literary Study of the Bible.*

(For the price upon their soul
Unto figures high doth roll
And must ever be passed by)
That, indeed, he should not die,
   Nor downward sight be casting:—
For the wise he sees Death call,
Fool and brute together fall—
They their wealth another race
Give; the inward thought they trace
   Is that, forever lasting,

Shall their houses ages view,
That their dwelling-places too
Generations safe shall stand;
Their own names they give their land.
   But man is not found staying
In the path of honor high;
He is like the beasts that die—
This, their way, is foolishness,
Yet, who after them shall press
   Approve the words they 're saying.

As a flock for Sheol, they
Are appointed; on their way
Their dread shepherd, Death, is found;
O'er them will the just be crowned
   Their rulers, in the morning—
And their beauty in its bloom
Sheol truly shall consume,
That for it no house may be;
But my soul will God set free,
   'Gainst power of Sheol warning.

He 'll receive me—not afraid
Do thou be, when rich one 's made,
When upon his house shall rise
Fame; he takes naught when he dies,—
   For, wealth with him descending,
Though he blessed his soul, though praise
Comes to one for selfish ways,
He 'll his fathers meet in night—
Honored, lacking mental sight,
   Like beast, to death man 's tending.

## PENITENCE

O GOD, have mercy upon me
    According to Thy love so kind;
According to Thy mercies free,
    In multitude beyond our mind.

In tenderness blot from Thy view
    Each one of my transgressions sore;
From mine iniquity, all through
    Wash me; o'er my sin cleansing pour.

For all my guilt is known by me;
    My sin reveals itself in might;
'Gainst Thee I 've sinned, 'gainst only Thee,
    And done this evil in Thy sight:

That Thou when speaking, justified
    May'st be; and when Thou judgest, clear—
Lo, in iniquity, inside
    My mother's womb did I appear.

In sin by her conceived was I—
    Behold Thou in each inward part
Desirest truth, and by-and-by
    Thou 'lt make me wise deep in my heart.

## PENITENCE

Purge me with hyssop; I 'll be clean:
  Wash me; I 'll whiter be than snow:
Thrill me with gladness, joy serene,
  So that the bones by Thee laid low

May yet rejoice. Ah! hide Thy face
  From all my sin; I have no pleas;
Enfold me in Thy wondrous grace,
  And blot out mine iniquities.

O God, create in me a heart
  All clean; a spirit steadfast make;
Me from Thy presence do not part,
  Nor from me Thy blest Spirit take.

The joy of Thy salvation old
  Do Thou unto my breast restore;
With a free spirit me uphold;
  Thy ways I 'll teach transgressors sore:

And sinners shall return to Thee—
  Me ransom from blood-guiltiness,
O God, Thou God who savest me;
  And loudly singing, Thee I 'll bless.

My tongue Thy righteousness shall sing;
  O Lord, my lips now open wide,—
And near and far my mouth shall fling
  Thy praise, while in Thy love I hide.

For Thy delight, in sacrifice
　　Is not: else would I give it Thee;
Burnt offering, before Thine eyes
　　A pleasant sight can never be.

The sacrifices of the Lord
　　A truly broken spirit are;
A broken, contrite heart, O God,
　　Thou 'lt not despise, though strayed afar.

Do good in Thy good pleasure now
　　To Zion, of the favored race;
Jerusalem's fair walls endow
　　With strength, and rear them in their place.

Then shalt Thou take supreme delight
　　In sacrifices borne to Thee,—
The sacrifices, glad and bright,
　　Of righteousness, from sin set free.

Burnt offering shall thrill Thine heart,
　　Also the whole burnt offering;
Then, bullocks it shall be their part
　　Unto Thine altar, Lord, to bring.

## THE KING'S PROTECTOR

O GOD, now hearken to my cry;
    Attend unto my prayer.
From earth's far ends to Thee will I
    Call, when my heart hath care.
Unto the Rock that is more high
    Than I—oh, lead me there.


To Thee, my Refuge, my heart clings,—
    Strong Tower from the foe,—
My way into Thy Tent me brings,
    Whence I will never go—
The blessed covert of Thy wings
    My refuge shall I know.


Thou God hast heard me vows proclaim;
    Thou hast bestowed on me
Their heritage who fear Thy name—
    The King long-lived shall be;
His years, prolonged by Thee, shall fame
    Of generations see.


Before God he shall e'er abide—
    Oh, loving-kindness warm

And truth to save him, Lord, provide:—
Thee will I praise in calm and storm;
Daily shalt Thou be magnified,—
So I 'll my vows perform.

## CALL TO PRAISE

MAY God to us His mercy show,
    And bless us with His grace;
Upon us cause His face to glow,—
    His benediction face.

That on the earth Thy way be known,—
    Thy saving health around
Among the nations all be shown,
    And in its might abound.

O let the peoples praise Thee, God,
    Let all the peoples praise;
O let the nations far abroad
    Glad songs in gladness raise.

The peoples Thou wilt judge in right,
    And all earth's nations lead—
O let the peoples with their might
    Praise Thee, our God, indeed.

Let all the peoples praise Thee now—
    Earth hath her increase borne:
God, our own God, shall us endow
    With blessings bright as morn.

God truly us shall richly bless,
And earth from far and near
Shall bow before His righteousness
In reverential fear.

## THE PRAISES OF THE KING

THY judgments, God, O give the King,
   And to his son Thy righteousness.
All righteous judgment shall he bring
   The people, and Thy poor he 'll bless
     With judgment strong.
The mountains to the people peace
   Shall bring; with righteousness be piled
The hills; in justice he 'll release
   The poor, and save each needy child,
     Though suff'ring long.

The tyrant he 'll to atoms break—
   They 'll fear Thee while endures the sun;
Yea, while the moon doth circuits make,
   While generations onward run,
     And onward still;
Like rain on new-mown grass he 'll fall,
   As showers that on the earth outpour;
And in his days, like palm-tree tall
   The righteous shall grow more and more;—
     And to the fill

Shall peace, Jehovah's peace, be found
   Until no more the moon shall rise;

He 'll rule the mighty world around:
  Before him the horizon flies
    Of sea and shore—
The river and the ends of earth
  Shall be the limits of his rule;
The dwellers in the desert's dearth
  Shall bow before his royal stool,
    And him adore.

His enemies shall lick the dust;
  The kings of Tarshish and the king
Of every isle shall to the just
  Their presents in profusion bring,
    And favor sue;
The kings of Sheba, Seba's crown,
  Shall offer gifts; before him all
The kings of earth shall bow them down;
  All nations at his feet shall fall,
    With service true.

For he shall save the needy soul,
  When from his throne he hears his cry;
The poor, on whom life's burdens roll,
  With none to lift them where they lie,
    No helping hand:
The poor and needy pities he;
  The needy souls who suffer woe
He'll place in strong security;
  Nor tyranny nor force shall know
    His happy band.

Dear shall their blood be in his sight;
  And they shall live; and he shall hold

## THE PRAISES OF THE KING

As gift, that only is his right,
   The wealth of Sheba's sparkling gold:
      And evermore
Men shall for him unite in prayer;
   Him shall they bless the whole day long;
Of corn they shall procure a share
   Upon the mountain-summits strong,—
      A bounteous store:

Its fruit like Lebanon shall shake:
   They whom the city walls immure,
Like grass, quick, springing growth shall make:
   His peace forever shall endure,
      And honored dwell
Long as the ever-shining sun:
   And men in him shall be all blest;
All nations as their course they run,
   In his true name obtaining rest,
      His joy shall tell.

Oh! blessedness, oh! blessedness
   Be his, Jehovah's, God, Most High,—
The God whom Israel doth bless,
   With whose great deeds no man can vie,—
      Our God and Friend.
Blest ever be His glorious name;
   His praise from all the earth be won—
Amen; and yet again the same.
   The prayers of David, Jesse's son,
      Are at an end.

# PRAYER FOR THE SHINING OF GOD'S FACE

GIVE ear, O Israel's Shepherd, kindly leading
  The tribe of Joseph, flock of Thine;
Dweller between the Cherubim, proceeding
  From Thee, let light abundant shine,
For Ephraim and Benjamin before Thy sight,
And for Manasseh, too, stir up Thy might.

Turn us again, O God! be Thy Face shining,
  And safety shall be ours from Thee.
Jehovah, God of mighty hosts, we're pining—
  How long, against Thy people's plea,
Against their prayer, shall rise the smoking of Thy wrath,
Far stirring desolation in their path?

Them hast Thou fed with bread of tears; them given
  Tears in great multitudes to quaff;
With strife, us from our neighbors Thou hast riven;
  Among themselves our foemen laugh—
Restore us now again, O God of myriad powers,
And cause Thy face to shine, and safety shall be ours.

# PRAYER FOR THE SHINING OF GOD'S FACE

A Vine from Egypt's land hast Thou been bearing;
   The natives that within the ground
Did plant it Thou did'st drive afar, preparing
   Room where it might entwine around.
It took deep root, and filled the surface of the land;
The mountains with its shadow-covering were
   spanned.

The boughs thereof God's cedars were resembling—
   She sent her branches to the sea;
Her little shoots within the breeze were trembling
   E'en where the River runneth free.
Why hast Thou broken down her fences, so that
   they
All pluck her, as they pass, each one, along the
   way?

The forest-boar doth ravage it, so greedy;
   The wild beasts feed on it, so bold:
Turn, turn again, O God of Hosts, we're needy;
   Look down from heaven, this Vine behold,
And visit it, Stock planted by Thy hand, time
   long,—
The Branch that for Thyself Thou madest strong.

Now 't is cut down; with fire indeed 't is burning;
   They perish, stricken by Thy face;
Let Thy right hand upon the man be turning,—
   The man who holds Thy right hand's place;—
Upon the son of man, by Thee with might arrayed,
Whom for Thyself, strong for all conflict Thou
   hast made.

So shall we not from Thee be backward straying.
   Awake us; on Thy name we 'll call—
Jehovah, God of Hosts, Thy love displaying,
   Turn us again, lift when we fall;
Upon our souls now cause Thy countenance to shine,
And safety shall be ours,—gift of Thy grace divine.

# THE JOYS OF GOD'S HOUSE

O LORD of Hosts, how passing fair
    Thy Tabernacles be!
How longs my soul to breathe their air,
    How faints their courts to see!
My heart and flesh cry out in prayer,
    O Living God for Thee.

Yea, hath the sparrow found a home,
    The swallow a safe nest,
Whence she will never want to roam,
    Where she may lay to rest
Her young ones,—'neath Thy sacred dome,
    Upon Thine altars blest.

O Lord of Hosts, my God, my King,
    How blest are they that dwell
Within Thy House! they still will sing
    Thy benedictions well.

Blest is the man whose strength is found
    In Thee, and in whose heart
The ways of holiness abound;
    Who makes a well to start
Within the vale of Baca's ground,—
    The pools with showers dart.

From strength to strength they onward pace;
　In Zion, one and all
Shall enter in before God's face—
　O Lord God, in whose presence fall
The hosts of heaven in their place,
　Attend unto my call.

O Jacob's God, give ear to me,
　Behold, O God, our Shield;
The face of Thine anointed see,—
　To him Thy glances yield.

Better a day Thy courts within
　Than thousand days elsewhere;
To bide beneath the tents of sin
　Is not my choice; my prayer
Is rather, far from earthly din,
　For Thine House-doors to care.

The Lord God is a Sun and Shield;
　He'll glory give and grace :
The upright ne'er in vain appealed
　For good before His face:
Those, Lord of Hosts, Thy love hath sealed
　Who trust in Thee shall place.

## LIFE AS A FLEETING DAY

JEHOVAH, Thou hast been our Habitation
   In all earth's generations long;
Before the mountains rose into their station,
   Or ever Thou had'st from the throng

Of atoms formed the earth, the world upraising,—
   Even from everlasting Thou
To everlasting art our God, whom praising,
   Before Thee shall creation bow.

Thou turnest man to dust, with cry: "Returning
   Be ye, the children of mankind."
A thousand years as yesterday discerning
   Art Thou, and they are left behind,—

Behind, like watch that one at night is keeping,
   Thou bearest them like swelling stream;
In their condition they are like the sleeping,—
   As those who wrapt in slumber dream.

At morning they are like the grass upgrowing—
   'T is flourishing and growing strong
At noontide's hour; at eventide man's mowing
   Has laid it dry the earth along.

For in Thine anger we 're consumed; we 're fretting
   At Thy deep wrath in trouble sore ;
Before Thee our iniquities Thou 'rt setting,—
   Our secret sins Thy sight before.

For in Thy wrath our days away are passing;
   Of our short years, the end appears.
They 're but a sigh; the sum of their amassing
   Is but threescore and ten brief years,

Or fourscore, maybe, through man's strength unshattered;
   Yet is their pride but toil and pain:
For soon 't is gone, and we in flight are scattered,—
   In face of death men strive in vain.

Who knows Thine anger's power; Thy wrath, according
   Unto the fear that 's due Thy name ?
So let us turn to count our days, affording,
   Time, Wisdom's heart that we may claim.

Return, O Lord, how long ? For each good servant
   Let it repent Thee; to us give
For Thine own mercy, satisfaction fervent
   At morning-tide, that we may live

Through all our days in joyfulness and gladness.
   O gladden us with joy serene
For days wherein Thou leddest us in sadness,—
   For years when evil we have seen.

## LIFE AS A FLEETING DAY

Before Thy servants let Thy work be glowing,—
 Thy glory on their children shine;
The beauty of the Lord be Thou bestowing
 On us,—the beauty all divine.

The work that with our hands we 've been performing
 Do Thou establish on us now;—
The work wherein our hearts are ever warming,—
This work of Thine,—establish Thou.

## THE LORD'S PAVILION

HE who within the secret place is hiding,
   Of God, the Lord Most High,
Beneath th' Almighty's shade shall be abiding,—
   His shelter ever nigh.

My Refuge and my Fortress I 'll be calling
   My Lord, the God I trust ;
Into the snare He 'll thee preserve from falling—
   God, ever kind and just.

And from the noisome pestilence thee keeping,
   He with His pinions thee
Shall cover; 'neath His wings safe sleeping,
   Blest shall thy refuge be.

His truth 's a shield and buckler: when there lieth
   Night's terrors round thy head,
Thou 'lt have no fear, and neither when there flieth
   The daytime's arrow dread.

Plague known to darkness shall not terrify thee,
   Nor fright shall thee attend
For noontide's fell destruction drawing nigh thee,
   Its wasting scourge to spend.

## THE LORD'S PAVILION

A thousand souls shall at thy side be falling,
    And close at thy right hand
Ten thousand more shall low be laid; but calling
    On God, thou safe shalt stand.

With thine eyes only shalt thou be beholding,—
    Their dark rewarding see
Who wicked are: for Thou, Lord, me art folding,
    My refuge sure, to be.

The Most High thou hast made thy habitation;
    No ill shall thee befall,
Nor any plague near thy tent take its station,
    And thee with fear appal.

For thee He 'll bid His angel hosts be caring,
    To keep thee all thy ways;
Thee, upward in their hands will they be bearing,
    Thy feet from stone-wounds raise.

On lion and on adder thou 'lt be treading,
    The lion's cub also ;
And serpent thou in nowise longer dreading,
    Thy feet shall trample low.

Deliverance I 'll be on him bestowing,
    Since he so loveth Me.
He, therefore, since My name he hath been knowing,
    Exalted high shall be.

Upon Me he shall day by day be calling,
    And I will answer him;
When Trouble's night upon his heart is falling,
    I 'll light its darkness dim.

Him I 'll deliver; honor bringing nigh him,
On him will I bestow ;
With length of days I 'll surely satisfy him;
Him My salvation show.

## THE LORD'S MAJESTY

JEHOVAH reigns; with majesty is He arrayed;
    Jehovah is apparelled fair and strong;
With strength He hath Him girded round; all
    firmly laid
Are the foundations that to earth belong.

No wind of universe the world can shake apart—
    Established firmly is Thy throne of old :
Thou, truly, from the everlasting ages art;
    Thy power through all the ages men behold.

The stormy floods have lifted up themselves, O
    Lord,
    The floods their voice have lifted very high,
The floods the deep sound of their roaring send
    abroad,
    Their mighty tumult rises to the sky.

Above the voices of the many waters loud,—
    The proud, resistless breakers of the sea,—
Jehovah, far on high, with might is sure endowed:
    The might that never flags nor fails hath He.

Sure, sure, beyond a doubt Thy testimonies live
    As strong to-day as in the days of yore:
To holiness, our lives, Jehovah, make us give;
    It well becomes Thine House forevermore.

## JEHOVAH'S WORTHINESS OF PRAISE

OH, come! oh, come! let us break forth in singing,
   In singing to the Lord;
A joyful, joyful noise let us be ringing
   Far, far the world abroad,—

To Him, our Rock, the Rock of our salvation.
   Before His presence now
Oh let us come with thankful celebration,
   Before Him humbly bow.

Let us a joyful noise to Him be raising,
   With psalm's pure melody;
For great, great is our God, the Lord we're praising,
   Above all gods is He.

Great King! Great King! in his sure hand He's shielding
   Earth's deepest places all;
The mountain heights are His,—Him homage yielding,
   Their Maker, Him they call.

## JEHOVAH'S WORTHINESS OF PRAISE 63

The sea, the sea is His; 't is He who made it;
  And with His gracious hands
He forméd the dry land, and so arrayed it
  That fair and strong it stands.


Oh come! oh come! in worship pure and lowly
  Let us before Him bend;
Low kneeling to the Lord, our Maker holy,—
  Our Maker and our Friend.


For He 's our God; to Him are we belonging;
  Yea, we His people are
Sheep of His hand, the flock His pasture thronging
  From folds both near and far.


To-day, oh that ye 'd hear His voice of pardon,—
  His voice that fain would bless!
Your heart, as at Meribah, do not harden,—
  As in the wilderness


In Massah's day, when, tried, your fathers straying
  All faithless, tempted Me,
Brought Me to proof, My precepts disobeying,
  And Mine own work did see.


Long, long, for forty years this generation
  Did grieve Me very sore;
I said: "It is a people weak; a nation
  Erring to their hearts' core.

"They have not known My ways." So was I
    swearing,
  By mighty wrath possessed,
That they the Promised Land should not be sharing,
  Nor come into My rest.

## JEHOVAH'S EXALTATION

JEHOVAH reigneth; be the earth rejoicing;
   Supremely glad
Let all the isles their jubilance be voicing,
   Nor more be sad.

Around about Him doth the darkness lower,
   And clouds, thick strown:
On righteousness and judgment rests in power
   His glorious throne.

A fire, devouring, flieth on before Him,
   And knows no bound,
Until it burneth (though they loud implore Him)
   His foes around.

His lightnings, in the darkened heav'ns assembled,
   The world did light:
The earth in fearfulness bowed down and trembled
   Before the sight.

The hills, like wax, were melted at the presence
   Of Him, the Lord;—
Before Him, who of power is the quintessence,
   The earth abroad.

The heavens, of His own righteousness the story
  In might declare:
And all the peoples have beheld His glory,
  Shed everywhere.

Ashamed be all who images are serving,
  Engraven, grim;—
That boast themselves of idols, from Jehovah
    swerving:
Ye gods, serve Him.

Heard Zion, and was glad, and Judah's daughters
  In joy did share,
For all Thy judgments, Lord, which Thou hast
    taught us
  In Thy strong care.

For Thou, Jehovah, art most high uplifted
  The earth above;
Above all gods with glory Thou art gifted,
  Thou God of love.

O ye that love the Lord, be evil hating:
  From wicked hands
He saves the souls of those, His pure ones, waiting
  On His commands.

Light for the righteous, sown in fields of sadness,
  Their gloom doth part;
And maketh He to bloom with flowers of gladness
  The upright heart.

Ye righteous, from Jehovah ever living
  Joy freely claim;
Praise ye, and magnify with high thanksgiving
  His holy name.

## JEHOVAH'S SALVATION

UNTO Jehovah sing
    A song before unknown;
For many a wondrous thing
    Hath He wrought for His own.

His right hand and His arm
    Of perfect holiness
Have rescued them from harm,
    And sin's enslaving stress.

The Lord hath made men see
    His true and saving might;
His righteousness hath He
    Shown in the nations' sight.

In memory doth He hold
    His mercy; faithfulness
That Israel did enfold,
    And all her house did bless.

Earth's distant ends have all
    Our God's salvation seen;
Upon Jehovah call,
    All earth in joyful pæan.

## JEHOVAH'S SALVATION

Break forth and sing for joy;
   Yea, glorious praises sing;
Praise for the Lord employ
   With harp of sweetest string,—

With harp, and with the voice
   Of truest melody;
With trumpet clear, rejoice;
   With cornet, tuneful be,—

Before the King, the Lord,
   Oh lift a joyful song;
Let ocean roar abroad,
   And those that in it throng—

The world, and they who dwell
   Upon its teeming lands;
Let all the floods joy tell
   With clapping of their hands.

Now let the mountains sing
   In joyous harmony;
Before Jehovah bring
   Praise that shall welcome be:

For He is coming,—He
   To judge the earth at length,—
The Lord of purity,
   And never-failing strength.

The world, in righteousness,
   Judged by the Lord shall be;
And He will surely bless
   The race with equity.

## THE REIGNING LORD

JEHOVAH reigneth over all;
    Let trembling on the people fall,
While they upon His mercy call.

Between the cherubim dwells He;
Be movéd earth, in reverence be
Adoring God's supremacy.

The Lord in Zion's hill is great;
Upon Him shall the peoples wait;
High o'er them all He's situate.

Thy terrible, Thy mighty name
Let them in glorious praise proclaim;
He's holy,—evermore the same.

The strength that dwelleth with the King
Doth judgment love, unfaltering;
To sturdy roots Thou makest cling

The plant of fairest equity;
Thou executest judgment free;
Thy righteousness shall Jacob see.

The Lord our God exalt ye high;
In worship at His footstool vie:
His holiness shall stand for aye.

Among His priests, on holy ground
Moses and Aaron, too, are found;
And with them who His praises sound

Is Samuel: God's grace they crave;
Upon His name, all strong to save,
They called, and He an answer gave.

Within the cloudy pillar, lo!
His accents strong He made them know;—
His favor unto them did show.

They kept the testimonies sure
He gave to them; His statutes pure
By them, unbroken, did endure.

O Lord, our God, to whom we bow,
Them with an answer surely Thou
Didst, from Thy gracious heart, endow.

Thou wast a God who didst bestow
Forgiveness that they all might know,
Who did to Thee for pardon go;—

Though, of their doings, Thou did'st take
Vengeance, e'en for Thy just name's sake,
Since they Thy pure commands did break.

The Lord our God exalt ye still,
And worship at His Holy Hill;
For He, our God, can ne'er do ill.

# A SONG OF THANKSGIVING

UNTO Jehovah sing with joy,
    All ye far-stretching lands;
Your hearts in gladsomeness employ
    While doing His commands.

Come to His presence ever blest
    With songs in sweet accord;
In this supreme assurance rest:—
    Jehovah—He is God.

'T is He, 't is He who hath us made;
    To Him do we belong:
We are His own; we're not afraid
    'Neath His protection strong.

We are His people; we the sheep
    Within His pasture fair:
Safe sheltered, He the souls doth keep
    Who trust His tender care.

Into His gates make entrance now,—
    Thank-off'rings in each hand;
Within His courts all lowly bow;
    In praise before Him stand.

To Him, to Him your thanks present,
  And ever bless His name
Whose love is thine o'ershadowing tent,
  Forevermore the same.

For good Jehovah is; all time
  His mercy doth endure;
His faithfulness in every clime,
  For every race, is sure.

## THE GOODNESS OF THE LORD

O SOUL of mine, Jehovah bless;
    And all that is in me
His name of perfect righteousness
    Still ever blessing be;
Jehovah's grace, my soul, confess,—
    His benefits so free:

Who doth forgive thine every sin;
    Thine every sickness heal;
Who, thee redeemed, thy heart within,
    Will never let thee feel
The pit's dark power, who thee doth win
    From woe to perfect weal;—

Who thee with loving-kindness long,
    And mercies tender, true,
Doth crown, and makes thy life a song;
    Who doth thy years endue
With good; so that like eagle strong
    Thou dost thy youth renew.

Jehovah worketh righteousness,
    And judgments, too, for those
Whom man unjustly shall oppress—
    His ways did He disclose
To Moses; Israel in distress,
    He guided 'gainst her foes.

The Lord's compassion is so great;
  Of grace He hath full store;
His anger through long time doth wait;
  His mercy's cup runs o'er—
He 'll chide not ever; soon or late,
  His wrath will be no more.

He hath not dealt to us the meed
  That all our sins require;
Nor hath rewarded us, indeed,
  With penalty entire
For our iniquities, but freed
  Us from chastisement dire.

As heav'n above the earth is high,
  So is His mercy free
Toward those who draw in reverence nigh
  His throne of purity—
Far as the east from western sky
  He makes our sins to be.

Like as a father pities, here,
  His children, God e'en so
Will pity them who Him shall fear—
  For He our frame doth know;
He minds that we are dust, yet dear
  To Him is man below.

For man, indeed, his days are grass;
  A flower of the field
He flourisheth.   The wind doth pass

## THE GOODNESS OF THE LORD

O'er it, and naught can shield
It from swift death; its place, alas!
No more shall be revealed.

But ages on, from year to year
    The mercy of the Lord
Will rest on them who Him shall fear;
    His righteousness is stored
For children's children, far and near;
    It is the blest reward

Of such as keep His covenant,
    And mind His words to keep,—
That He to them will surely grant.
    His throne Jehovah deep
And strong within the heav'ns doth plant;
    His realm hath world-wide sweep.

O bless the Lord, His angels all:
    Ye strong, and full of might,
On whom, attent, His Word doth fall;
    Ye, ever in his sight—
Ye hosts of His, in blessing call
    Upon the Lord of Light;—

His servants all, below, on high,
    Whose will He doth control—
All works of His, in earth and sky,
    Where farthest planets roll,—
Yea, farther than our thoughts can fly:—
    Oh bless the Lord, my soul.

## A SONG OF THE REDEEMED

OH give thanks unto the Lord: for He is good:
    His mercy doth endure forevermore.
Let God's redeemed say so, who safe have stood,—
    Whom saved He from their adversary sore,
And from the lands did bring them where He would—
    From east, west, north, and ocean's pathway o'er.

They roamed a lone way in the wilderness;
    They found no city where they might abide—
Hungry were they and thirsty; in sharp stress
    Their soul within them fainted. Then they cried
To God in their affliction, them to bless;
    And He from pain to healing them did guide.

He led them also by a pathway straight,
    That they might find a city of abode;—
O would that men, e'en for His goodness great,
    Would praise the Lord,—for works that He hath showed
All wonderful to them that on Him wait,—
    That He upon mankind hath free bestowed.

For He the longing soul doth satisfy;
    The hungry soul with good things doth He fill.

Those who beneath the veil of darkness lie,
  Those who are covered by Death's shadow chill,—
Because against God's words they raised a cry,
  Rebellious, seeking not to do His will,—

Because the plan of God Most High they held.
  In cool contempt: then He their heart brought down
With toil; they helpless fell who had rebelled:
  Then, crying from the waves that them would drown,
God saved them, led them out, for them expelled
  The dark death-shade that on their way did frown.

Their lands, also, He broke asunder far—
  O would that men, e'en for His pure, good ways,
Would praise the Lord,—for works that wondrous are,
  Toward children of mankind: Him let men praise!
For He the gates of brass hath rent ajar,
  Cut iron bars that strong themselves did raise.

Fools for the way of their transgression are
  Afflicted, and by reason of their sin—
All kinds of meat their soul repels afar;
  The gates of death they almost enter in—
Unto the Lord they cry when pain their lives doth bar,
  And He, from woe, for them doth safety win.

His Word He sends, and them doth healing bring;
   He them delivers from destruction fell—
O that men to the Lord would praises sing
   For all his wonders nigh incredible,—
His goodness to mankind in everything;—
   O that men would Jehovah's praises tell,

And sacrifices of thanksgiving free
   Be theirs; His works with song let them declare.
They that go down in ships unto the sea,
   They that for trade the mighty waters dare,
These see Jehovah's works, how great they be,—
   His wonders that the vasty deep doth bear.

For He but speaks, and stormy winds arise,
   Which lift in might each darkly gathering wave;—
They mount, they mount in grandeur to the skies,
   Again they sink in deepest ocean-grave—
Because of pain, their soul all melting sighs,
   Like drunkard reeling, help they wildly crave.

They stagger, e'en at their wits' end indeed—
   Then, in their woe, unto the Lord they cry;
And them from their distresses doth He lead,
   The stormy sea, now calm He makes to lie:
So, glad, because from tumult they are freed,
   He brings them to the port for which they sigh.

O that men for His goodness great the Lord
   Would praise, and for His works of wonder rare
Which freely to mankind He doth afford;

# A SONG OF THE REDEEMED

Let them exalt Him in th' assembly where
The people come; to Him be praise outpoured,
   By them who 're seated in the elders' chair.

He turneth rivers to a wilderness
   And water-springs into a thirsty ground;—
Rich land to land where salt is in excess,
   E'en for the wickedness that doth abound
In them that dwell therein, whose guilt doth press,
   And call for punishment the region round.

The wilderness He makes a pool of rain,
   To water-springs He turneth the dry land;
He makes the hungry in its bounds remain,
   That there a city of abode their hand
May fashion, and sow fields of waving grain,
   And vineyards plant, and more and more expand,

That they may get them fruits that shall not cease;
   He blesseth them, so that they 're multiplied;
He suff'reth not their cattle to decrease.
   Again, they 're minished, and bowed low abide,
Because of pain, oppression, sorrow; peace
   Has vanished from its station at their side.

Contempt upon the princes doth He pour,
   And causeth them to wander in the waste
Where no way can be found, its surface o'er.
   Yet He the needy one on high hath placed,
So that affliction he may feel no more;
   With flock of little ones his home hath graced.

The upright shall behold it, and be glad;
   And all Iniquity her mouth shall close.
Whoso is found with Wisdom's vesture clad
   Shall to these things give heed where'er he goes;
The mercies of the Lord, that he has had,
   He 'll think upon,—e'en how his need God knows.

## THE IDEAL KING

JEHOVAH said unto my Lord, "Be sitting
　　　At My right hand;
Until I make Thy foes Thy footstool fitting
　　　By My command."

The Lord the rod of Thy strength shall be sending
　　　From Zion blest:
Rule Thou amongst Thy foes in power unending,
　　　Victor confessed.

Thy people in the day Thy power prevaileth
　　　Themselves present
Freely: in beauty that no sinning paleth;
　　　With heart unrent

By strife, Thou hast from out the womb of morning
　　　The dew of youth.
The Lord hath sworn; He'll not repent; adorning
　　　Thy Church with truth.

Thou art, like to Melchizedek, forever
　　　A glorious Priest.
The Lord beside Thee kings from might shall
　　　sever,—
　　　　His wrath released.

He will be Judge among the nations, chilling
    Their hearts with dread;
The places with the dead shall He be filling;
    E'en through the head

Lands, far and near He 'll strike, before Him shrinking ;
    Their strongholds rift;—
Therefore shall He—from wayside streamlet drinking—
    The head uplift.

## HALLELUJAH SONG

WHEN forth from Egypt Israel went,
    When from a people of strange speech
Away the house of Jacob bent
    Their footsteps, other fields to reach,—

Judah became His holy seat
    And His dominion Israel;
The sea beheld and beat retreat,
    Yea, Jordan's waves that wildly swell.

The mountains skipped like rams around,
    The little hills like new-born sheep.
O Sea, what ails thee; why art found
    Far fleeing, O thou raging Deep?

Jordan, what aileth thee, that thou
    Should'st from thy course take backward way?
What ails ye, mountains, too, that now
    Like rams ye should be skipping gay?

What ails ye, little hills, that ye
    Like new-born sheep should sport around?—
Earth, tremble, thou! for near to thee
    The Lord, the mighty Lord is found.

Tremble! for Jacob's God is near,
Who turned the rock abiding long
Into a pool of water clear,
The flint into a fountain strong.

# JEHOVAH'S LOVING-KINDNESS

I LOVE the Lord, since He hath heard
    My voice, my supplication strong:
Since He hath marked my every word,
    I 'll call on Him my whole life long.

The cords of death my heart did bind,
    And Sheol's pains took hold on me;
Trouble and sorrow did I find,
    Nor from their grasp could set me free.

Then called I on Jehovah's name:
    "I pray Thee, save my soul, O Lord;"
The Lord is gracious, aye the same,
    And righteous is His name adored.

For mercy, too, our God is known;
    The Lord the simple soul doth keep:
I low was brought, and He alone
    Delivered me in trouble deep.

My soul, return unto thy rest;
    For bounteously the Lord with thee
Hath dealt,—attentive to thy quest;
    His grace is boundless as the sea.

For Thou hast saved my soul from death;
   Mine eyes from tears; my feet made stand:
Before the Lord while I have breath
   I 'll walk within the fair life-land.

I well believed when thus I spake:
   With great afflictions spent was I:
And hasty speech my tongue did make:
   All men I said but live a lie.

To God what shall I offer up
   For all his benefits toward me?
I now will take salvation's cup,
   And calling on God's name I 'll be.

My vows unto the Lord of Light
   I 'll pay, where Israel worshippeth.
How precious in Jehovah's sight
   The triumph of His saints in death!

O Lord, I am Thy servant true,—
   Thy servant, son of thine handmaid;
Sundered hast Thou my chains in two—
   My loving thanks to Thee 'll be paid,

And on Jehovah's name I 'll call;
   I 'll pay my vows unto the Lord,
Where, worshipping, His people fall,—
   His people gathered from abroad.

I 'll worship in Jehovah's courts;
   In thee, Jerusalem, I 'll raise
My song, O fairest of resorts!—
   Unto the Lord, now give ye praise.

## SONG OF THE EXILE

IN my distress I raised a cry
   Unto the Lord; He answer gave.
  From lying lips my soul, God save,
And from the tongue that plans to lie.

What shall be given unto thee?
   What shall be done to thee still more,
    Thou tongue, whose lies are planned before,
That speakest e'er deceitfully?

Sharp arrows of the sons of might,
   With coals of juniper aglow.
    That I should bide in Mesech,—woe!—
In Kedar's tent, prepared for fight!

My soul hath had for many a day
   To dwell with him that hateth peace.
    For peace was I; for strife's surcease:
But when I speak, for war are they.

# THE HILLS OF GOD

TO God's fair hills I 'll lift mine eyes:
   From whence shall come mine aid?
My help e'en from the Lord shall rise,
   Who heav'n and earth hath made.

Thy foot He never will permit
   In helplessness to fall:
Thy Keeper thee will never quit,
   Nor list to slumber's call.

Lo, He that keepeth Israel
   Shall slumber not, nor sleep.
Jehovah, God, forever well
   Thy waiting soul doth keep:—

The Lord 's thy shade on thy right hand—
   The sun thee shall not smite
By day, and safely shalt thou stand
   Beneath the moon by night.

God, from all evil, thee shall win;
   He 'll cover thy soul o'er—
Thy going out and coming in
   He 'll keep forevermore.

# THE PILGRIM SALUTING JERUSALEM

HOW glad was I when comrades said,
    Let us the blessed pathway tread
  Unto Jehovah's Temple fair!
Within thy gates our weary feet
Have stood, Jerusalem complete,—
  Jerusalem, of beauty rare!

A city thou that builded art
Strong and compact in every part,
  Whereto the tribes their footsteps bend;—
The tribes with whom the Lord doth dwell
For witness unto Israel,—
  Who to Jehovah's Word attend.

They go their thankful songs to bring
Unto their gracious Lord and King—
  For there are thrones for judgment placed,—
Thrones that in David's House are found.
Pray that God's peace may compass round
  Jerusalem, with beauty graced.

Prosperity shall be for them
That love thee, blest Jerusalem—
  Within thy walls let peace abide;

Within thy palaces serene
Prosperity be ever seen,
  Nor harm nor sorrow thee betide.

E'en for my brethren's sake, indeed,—
E'en for mine own companions' need,
  The greeting that I now will speak
Is: Peace in thee be richly stored
For His fair House,—the Lord our God—
  Thy good I'll diligently seek.

## THE EXILE'S PRAYER

TO Thee I raise mine eyes afar
   O Thou that dost the heav'ns command.
Behold, as eyes of servants are
   Directed to their master's hand,

As eyes of maiden steadfast rest
   Upon the mistress she obeys,—
So, on Jehovah ever blest
   Our eyes in patient longing gaze,

Till He upon us mercy show.
   Have mercy, mercy on us Lord:
Contempt our soul doth overflow,
   From hand of enemies outpoured.

Our soul is filled exceedingly
   With scorning very fierce and loud
Of those who at their ease still be;
   And with contempt of all the proud.

## THE EXILE'S MEDITATION

HAD not the Lord been on our side, unfailing,
  Let Israel now say;
Had not the Lord been on our side, prevailing
  When men opposed our way,—

Then us, while yet alive, would they have swallowed,
  When blazed for us their wrath;
Then had the waves to whelm us pressing, followed
  And overflowed our path.

Then had the stream—proud stream—our soul
    gone over.
  Jehovah God be blest,
Who gave us not unto the hostile rover
  Who would our soul have pressed.

Our soul, like bird from fowler's snare is flying:
  The snare breaks; flight we take.
Upon Jehovah's name we are relying,
  Who heav'n and earth did make.

# THE STRENGTH OF ZION

THEY who in God Jehovah trust
   Are even as Mount Zion strong,
  Which standeth through the ages long,
Unmoved, nor crumbleth into dust.

E'en as around Jerusalem
   The hills in strength and beauty lie,
  So round His own the Lord Most High
Remaineth—aye, to shelter them.

Sceptre of them that wicked be
   Shall rest not on the just one's lot;
  That they their righteous hands may not
Put forth unto iniquity.

Do good, O Lord, do good to those
   That be good, and to them that are
  Upright in heart, and turning far
From all who righteousness oppose.

But as for those who good repel
   In crooked ways,—these God shall lead
  With them of many a wicked deed.
Peace, peace abide on Israel!

## SOWING AND REAPING

WHEN Zion's hard captivity
    Jehovah kindly turned again,
We were like them that dreaming be,—
Then was our mouth with laughter stored,
    Our tongue was full of songful strain.
Then said they through the race abroad,

"The Lord great things for them hath done."
    He greatly blessed us; glad we are—
Lord, turn again each captive one,
As streams that in the southland flow.
    They who while shedding tears afar
Through all the fields and meadows sow,

In joy, at harvest-time shall reap;
    Though on his way he goes along,
And while he bears the seed doth weep,
Though now he worn and weary grieves,
    He'll come again, with joyful song,
The while he bringeth in his sheaves.

## SONG OF HOME

EXCEPT the house be builded by
   The Lord, its builders vainly toil:
The city kept not 'neath God's eye,
   Though watched all night, will man despoil.

Vain 't is for you that you arise
   So early, and take rest so late;
And eat the bread that labor buys:
   Sleep makes He on His loved ones wait.

Lo, children are a heritage
   That come, in favor, from the Lord;
The fruit the womb of every age
   Shall bear, is His own blest reward.

As arrows in a strong man's hand,
   So, children sprung from youthful stem.
With happiness the life is spanned
   Of him whose quiver 's full of them.

To them, indeed, shall come no shame,
   E'en when their foes for them shall wait,
And they shall with them converse claim,—
   Their enemies within the gate.

# THE BLESSED HOME

BLEST truly are all they that fear
    The Lord, and walk within His ways.
    For what thy hands by toiling raise
Thou 'lt eat for sustenance and cheer.

Thou shalt be happy, and with thee
    It shall be well: as for thy wife,—
    Like to a vine of fruitful life
Within thy house she 'll ever be.

Thy children like rich plants shall grow,—
    Like olive-plants, thy table round—
    Behold, that blessed shall be found
The man who fear of God doth know.

Thee, out of Zion God shall bless:
    And thou, through all life's many days
    Upon Jerusalem shall gaze,
Beholding all its blessedness.

Yea, thou with thine own eyes shalt see
    The children of a later race,—
    Thy children's children through, God's grace.
Peace, peace on Israel resting be!

# THE PENITENT EXILE

FROM out the depths to Thee, O Lord
    I've cried; my voice, Jehovah, hear:
Thine ears be now attentive toward
    My voice; Thy suppliant be Thou near.

If Thou man's sins, Lord, marking be,
    Who, then, Jehovah, who shall stand?
But there's forgiveness full with Thee,
    That Thou may'st righteous fear command.

I for Jehovah wait; doth wait
    My soul, and hope I in His Word—
Looks early for the Lord and late
    My soul, with earnest longing stirred—

More, more than watchmen for the morn
    Look through the night with eager eyes;
Yea, more than watchmen, till be torn
    Night's veil, and morning's sun doth rise.

Hope, hope ye in Jehovah blest,
    O ye His people, Israel!
Unto the Lord make full request—
    His mercy is a springing well.

His mercy 's free; with Him is found
Redemption, plenteous as the rain—
For Israel cleansing shall abound
From Him, for every sinful stain.

# MEDITATION ON SIMPLICITY

HAUGHTY is not my heart, O Lord,
  Nor raised in loftiness mine eyes;
Nor let I things of great emprise
Work for my energies afford;

Nor do I let myself be wiled
  By things too high; I 've quieted
  My soul, and stillness round it shed
Like mother with a weanéd child.

Peace on my soul dost Thou outpour;
  Like weanéd child, my soul 's with me.
  In God, O Israel, hoping be
From this time forth, forevermore.

# ELEGY OF THE CAPTIVITY

WHERE Babylon's fair streams were flowing,
   There we sat down; yea, there we wept;—
When we in mind to Zion going
   Thought of our home before us kept.

Upon the willows, river-shading,
   Our harps we hung, the banks along,
For there our lords, our woe invading,
   Asked us their captives for a song:

And they who tore our hearts all tender
   Required that mirthful we should be;
And cried: "Now we would have you render
   A song of Zion's melody."

The Lord's own song!—How can it yet be
   That we should sing it far from home?
Jerusalem! if I forget thee
   While in captivity I roam,

Be my right hand her skill forgetting;
   And to one spot my tongue adhere
If o'er all joy I be not setting
   Jerusalem, in radiance clear.

'Gainst Edom's children be recalling
  That day, Lord, of Jerusalem;
When, " Rase it! " cried they; " now be falling
  Its basal stones; yea, scatter them."

Daughter of Babylon, for wasting,
  For fell destruction set aside,—
Be happy he who thee is hasting
  To woe that for thy guilt shall bide,—

As thou ourselves one time wert serving;
  Be happy he that with hard shock
Thy children takes, with strength unswerving,
  And dasheth them against the rock.

## THE AVENGING LORD

THE Lord who is my Rock be blest,
  Who trains my hands for war's behest,—
My fingers for the fight.
My Goodness and my Fortress He,
My Tower high; He rescues me;
  He is my shield of might.
In Him I trust for every hour;
He makes my people feel my power,
  Submissive in my sight.

Lord, what is man that he should find
Such knowledge of him in Thy mind!
  Or what the son of man
That Thou should'st make account of him!
Like vanity, he's light and dim,—
  A shadow is his span.
Thy heavens bow, O Lord; come down
And simply touch each mountain's crown,—
  They'll smoke beneath Thy ban.

Thy lightning from the sky cast forth,
And scatter them from south and north;
  Shoot out Thine arrows swift—
Destroy them; let Thy hand descend
And save me; in wild waves defend;

And kindly me uplift
From strangers' snares: their mouth is vain,
Their right hand's way is never plain,
   But makes to falsehood drift.

A new song unto Thee I 'll sing;
My psaltery for Thee I 'll bring,—
   My ten-stringed instrument.
I 'll gladly utter praise to Thee.
Who safety gives to kings? 'T is He;
   He David saves; and bent
Shall be the sword that him would bruise.
O save us, and strange foes confuse
   Whose mouth to sham is lent,—

Whose right hand is a false right hand.
When all our sons throughout the land
   Shall be as young plants grown;
When all our daughters, too, shall be
As corner-stones, most fair to see,
   By palace ne'er outshone;
When all our garners full, run o'er,
Affording every kind of store
   That husbandmen can own;

When lambs by thousands shall be born,
And tens of thousands shall adorn
   Our fields with snowy fleece;
When all our oxen shall have strength
To labor, though it be at length;

When breakings-in shall cease;
When there be no outgoing feet,
Nor mur'ring sounds in any street,
For plaints shall yield to peace:—

Great happiness, indeed, hath place
With people found in such a case;
Their joys no more shall wane.
Yea, happy are the people who
Choose Him who 's ever just and true,
Who blessing brings from bane.
Happy are they who 've Him adored,
Happy the race whose God 's the Lord
Who evermore shall reign.

## CREATION'S PRAISE

HALLELUJAH ! praise the Lord,—
   From the heav'ns His praises sing:
Let His praises be outpoured;
   In the heights now let them ring.

Ye, His Angels, speak His praise:
   Praise Him, all His Hosts on high:
Praise Him, Sun and Moon, upraise
   Praise to God who cannot die:

Praise Him, all ye Stars of Light,
   Heav'ns of heav'ns, His praises tell:
And ye Streams, beyond our sight,
   Let them praise God's name right well:—

For He uttered His command,
   And they were created all
He hath set them with His hand
   So they never-more shall fall.

He hath made a sure decree
   Which shall men forever keep—
From the earth God praiséd be:
   Praise Him, Dragons in the deep;

Fire and Hail and Vapor, Snow;
   Stormy Wind that doth His word;
Mountains and the Hills below,
   That with strength His hand doth gird;

Fruitful Trees, and Cedars too;
   Beasts and Cattle everywhere;
Creeping Things, Fowl flying through
   And swiftly wafted in the air;

Kings and Peoples of the earth;
   Earthly Princes, Judges all;
Youths and Maidens, full of mirth,
   Aged Men and Children small:—

Let them praise Jehovah's name,
   For His name alone is high;
And His glory, e'er the same,
   Is above the earth and sky.

He hath lifted up the horn
   Of the people of His love;
Praise hath God, Jehovah,—borne
   From His saints to Him above;—

E'en of Israel so dear,—
   People whom He loved right well,—
People to Jehovah near:
   Praise the Lord, Immanuel.

## THE PRAISES OF THE SAINTS

PRAISE ye the Lord: unto Jehovah sing
    A glad new song;
Among His saints now let His praises ring
    In rapture strong.

Let Israel in his Creator blest
    All joyful be:
Let Zion's children in their King take rest
    In gladness free:

His name, let them in joyous dancing praise
    And magnify:
With timbrel and with harp let them upraise
    His praises high.

For true enjoyment doth Jehovah take
    E'en in His own;
The meek, fair with salvation will He make
    From His bright throne.

Joyful in glory, let the saints of earth
    Uplift their heads:
Let them their songs upraise with hearty mirth
    Upon their beds.

Within their mouth let God's high praises be
  With strength outpoured,
And in their hand let them be wielding free
  A two-edged sword:—

Upon the heathen nations to command
  Vengeance all stern,
And punishments on them who from God's hand
  To evil turn;

To bind their kings with chains they cannot break,
  Nor soon discard,
And for their nobles suffering to make
  With fetters hard;

On them to see that judgment just shall fall
  In writing stored:—
This honor have His holy people all—
  Praise ye the Lord.

# FINALE

O BLESSED Lord, to whom the choir
    Of Angels bring their sweetest song;
Whose Heart of Love can never tire
    Of loyal praise the ages long:—
Accept these lays, from Thine own Word,—
    A never-failing Treasury brought:
And through Thy grace, where'er they 're heard,
    Be Thy pure ways more purely sought.

May Thine own Singers of the Past
    Through these new songs new honors gain;
Thy truth through them be held more fast;
    Thy changeless love appear more plain.
Blend with their halting harmony
    Chords of the music all divine;
Let them be sung with fervor free
    By hearts uplifted, Lord, to Thine.

Let Thy blest Spirit bring them near
    The souls by sin and care distressed;
Their melody the faithless fear,
    The restless passion sing to rest:
Their notes of deathless joy and praise
    Let Thy redeemed ones make their own,
While they their glad thanksgiving raise
    To Thee who sittest on the throne.

www.ingramcontent.com/pod-product-compliance
Lightning Source LLC
Chambersburg PA
CBHW021942160426
43195CB00011B/1193